Poems on the Paintings of Kandinsky

Nick Monks

I0203379

Bluebell Publishing

For Amanda, Karl, Saskia

Title Page

Poems on the Paintings of Kandinsky- Nick Monks

Published July 2020

Printed by Lulu

www.lulu.com

ISBN 978-1-9163546-9-2

CONTENTS

PREFACE

Wassily Kandinsky 16th December 1866 to 13th December 1944. Was a Russian painter and art theorist. One of first abstract artist pioneers.

He was born in Moscow. Spent his childhood In Odessa, Crimea. Studied law and economics In Moscow and was successful. Began painting studies at the age of 30.

In 1896 he settled in Munich. Studying at the Academy of Fine Arts. Returned to Moscow in 1914. And was in involved in a culture role after the Russian revolution. Then at odds with socialist realism.

Returned to Germany Where he taught at the Bauhaus from 1922 until the Nazis closed it in 1933. Lived the rest of his life in France, where he died in 1944 in Neuilly Sur Seine. In 2016 Christies auctioned Kandinsky's painting *Ridged and Bent* for $23.3 million.

Poems on the Paintings of Kandinsky

Paysage Avec Pont

Painted before he became more abstract.

Water, an appealing wash of whites and blues.

Thick textured brush strokes

A white bridge. Appealing like cold manufactured marble.

Green mountains. Nobody here. A reflection troubled vibrant-

In the water. Destitute beauty. A house by the shore.

Where you'd like to live

Slippage of paint. Brusque creativity. Chink of pink sky.

An aloneness. A bruised painting. Were the colours long to be free

In abstraction. And escape the representational

Moscow Cityscape

A topsy turvy city. Twisted and remade in an explosion-

of blues and purples.

A city surveyed and measured. Poverty and wasted life's,

Destitution and the disabused. The vice and bullying and injustice.

All in gods own land sideways

Upside down. On the edge. Play. Escape. Carousel.

Kandinsky tames New York. Here paints Moscow.

Play skyscrapers. Play cathedrals.

Wobbly real-estate with jist. Non discernible shapes as existents

A sun rays. Rainbows. Light exaltations. Shopping for truth.

Magnificent. In excelsis.

Brownish

Grey brown desert. A camel rendered stylized shape. Red blood sun or moon. Black night. Four appealing lines white diagonal from red and grey base. Flag arrangement. The simplicity of the stylized desert is beautiful. A place were dreams become as pure as rendered prayer. Were wishes wither in death sun. Skeletal. A barren abandoned triangle that could be a pyramid. Black night. Illuminated desert. Mirrored. An echo in the barren. A desert baptism. Vultures over the skeletal bones. Sleep at night in the desert homecoming. Under bouquets of crystal- clear ice- cold stars. Walk forever in searing heat.

Colour Study: Squares with Concentric Circles

Intense little suns. Exuberant rare exotic flowers. Good news flown in from carrier pigeon. Kaleidoscope ponds. 12 studies of geometric circles and squares. A dawn.

Scintillating make up. A child's genius in year 2 of infant school. 12 suns each original. Saved from black holes and becoming nebulae. By a painter collector of suns. Circles and squares dressed for the evening palace ball. Verdant colour- scapes of the souls of cities.

Announcement 1

A bath of colours. Yellow wheat field road. Inexplicable blocks of colours- rendered . A solid large detached house. Partially obliterated by two green trees. Echo's sonic beeps of colours. A sky rendered abstract.

Yellow wheat road I follow. Away from the abstract. Into geometric lines and shapes of later paintings. Live in this house. As you open the door. A mathematician in love with yellow, pink, blue, green. Has created a new world. Were form and line and colour have escaped the representational.

Munich

A group of people outside of the conurbation of Munich. In cotton buds cauliflower of red green and blue. The church of saint Ursula in the city skyline. Steel blue deep sky. Buildings substantive yellow, blue, green. As the surroundings become abstract. And six people small cavort at something mysterious and undefined. In the wool scape far beyond the city gates.

The Blue Rider 1

A person in a blue cape. Galloping on a white horse with red bridle over the deadened joy. Of decaying still autumn. Trees in orange on the hill summit. The grasses and bracken yellow and light green/blue. The dash will arrive nowhere. As the painting is frozen. Who would wish to be anywhere else than in the silence of hill and wind movement. Galloping free. To nowhere across autumnal beauty.

Already the air is cool. Soon the bite of winter. Fleet escape. Hurried gallop. Summer has gone. And the blue cape wisps with the speed. Of tomorrows. The hills magnetic allure of colours. A glimpse of the pale rider over the decaying autumn foliage. Deep forests beyond the hills contours. A galant sea of a sky. The fervid sail of horse and blue rider.

Blue Mountain

Horse riders galloping on rearing horses at the meadow foot of a blue mountain. Two trees one pink. One yellow dance in gigantic size on each side of the mountain. And the sky is a pastel light firework display. And the blue mountain fizzles in blue. The three riders and onlookers. Riding to the exotic castle beneath the blue mountain. Were for generations the tribe gazed at the peaks towering symmetry. A mountain mystique of promise. Marriages were played out. Wars fought. Celebrations enacted. And two trees in the fertile meadow foothills. Below the majestic mountain. The horses hoof falls.

Das Bunte Leben

Palace on a high hill. Entwined exotic people. Talking to each other and passers -by. Playing music. In a wash of blue that could be the night dusk. On a polka dot blue park. With the delicious sea in the background. Chatter and revelry. A wilderness of peoples. Perhaps the end of a major war. At the end of the day. They chatter and cavort. To become citizens of the blue jewelled land.

House at Murnau, 1908

Houses with bright colours. Sun playing on the curved street. Dark blue shadows. No one around in the town. Walls seep and loose shape. Well tendered houses. Nobody lives here. The houses are empty. In pale colours. Becoming paint not copies of a street. Deep blue sky. Moving to abstraction. Colour flashes freed. To make a becoming.

In Blue

A red sun bleeding. Slithers of red carrot

Black ice triangle

A triangle stick with an eye window

Deep sonorous blue. Layered with syntax and affect

Other shapes vying trying to be symmetrical

A roof top song

A melody into the unknown rendered.

The Blue Rider Poster

A group of artists who rejected the Neue Kunstlervereinigung Munchen in Munich. As too strict and traditional. Included Russian emigrants Wassily Kandinsky/ Alexej von Jawlensky/ Marianne von Werefkin.

And native Germans such as Franz Marc/August Macke/ Gabriele Munter

Similar- to *Die Brucke* 1905. Important to expressionism. The Blue Rider group lasted from 1911 to 1914

The poster/ magazine cover by Kandinsky shows a white and blue patched horse and mythic rider. The horse rearing. And perhaps a king or prince. With ceremonial cap. Riding to the future.
The title Der Blaue Reiter to the side. In a large white shape. And a black background to the painting.

Succession

A musical score of appealing brightly coloured shapes. Each comes after the other. Till there are just lines and dots.

Thus our path through life is incomprehensible. And stunningly beautiful. Haunted by enchantment. Each figure of squiggle a form that isn't in the natural world. An exclamation mark of joy and pain.

Autumn 11

Let the earth be yellow. Let it bathe beautifully. A mirrored reflection in water. Yellow fish in a green ocean. Yellow sand. Bright.

Of high buildings or sails. Blocks of blue and green and red. Will do for a modern sky.

The colours have become separated from Rembrandt's or Vermeer's paintings. And float like delicious treacle or cinnamon. In an acrid world of beauty called home.

Park of St Cloud, Autumn 1906

A fecund musky with beech kernels forest floor. Here badgers and weasels would roam beneath red squirrel and chaffinch and coal tit.

Strange fruits on the trees. The crop of total wars carnage. And civilian executions. Dappled arrayed colours. Leaf's like a thousand green flags.

A childhood mystique. The enchantment of being lost. Flashes of red and pink truffles on the soil or crab apples or suns shadow and light gifts. As we tarry then walk through into the lake and pond under a fizzling blue sky. From between the trees.

Transverse Line, 1923

Geometrical Pythagorean geometry. A pale cream background. To complex logical equations on being. Suns rainbows flags in plenty. Dissected by mathematical lines. Order and sometimes despair. One thousand paintings on one canvass. Start again with a world traipsed by rings. Other planets. Lines of different types. A map of life and our environment, world and galaxy. A playground exactitude.

Schwabing Nicolaiplatz, 1902

Village houses nestled in an unknown village you travelled through to get to the city. The field sequestered in snow. Thick brushstrokes render the homes of the villagers.

Paths of footfall across the snow field. Trees to the side. The village is impenetrable but scenic. What is there of revelry here or art endeavour. Looking askance at the city smog. And degeneracy. The rendered scape hurts somehow. The village is given the gift of being created. And existing with beautiful snow on a gallery wall.

Winter Landscape 11

When snow fall comes. Deep cascading meandering blue. We
shudder pleasurably in our deep sleep . if snow is white. Then it
should be rendered blue/yellow/orange/green. To sequester the
very cold stillness-

Of a village where Robert Frost lived. And charted a man a woman.
And the entwined hope of an eternal village. The energic vibe of
Brixton and Handsworth, Birmingham and downtown Detroit and
Chicago. Also with red snow.

Untitled

A vortex of despair and hope. An alien and familiar fantastical world. Shape-dom. Semi circles concentric. Red exhalations. Green fields. Unsettling focus. The faulty or accurate photograph of Los Angeles. Undone. A beautiful esoteric creation. Shapes of colours over cream. Paths rendered.

The World Map

Series1

12

Powered by Bing

www.ingramcontent.com/pod-product-compliance
Lightning Source LLC
Chambersburg PA
CBHW022041090426
42741CB00007B/1161